THE WAR THAT STILL GOES ON

THE WAR THAT STILL GOES ON

Adapted from
Thucydides' History of the Peloponnesian Wars
and Plato's Dialogue with Alcibiades
by John Barton

OBERON BOOKS
LONDON

First published in 2006 by Oberon Books Ltd
521 Caledonian Road, London N7 9RH
Tel: 020 7607 3637 / Fax: 020 7607 3629
e-mail: info@oberonbooks.com
www.oberonbooks.com

A catalogue record for this book is available from the British
Library.

ISBN: 9781840026511

Characters

THUCYDIDES

PERICLES

CORCYRAN

CORINTHIAN

1ST ATHENIAN

2ND ATHENIAN

SPARTAN KING

BRASIDAS

CLEON

DIODOTUS

MELIAN

ALCIBIADES

SOCRATES

NICIAS

CAMARINAEAN

GYLIPPUS

The numbered 'scenes' are suggestions only.
The piece should run as continuous action.

(Prologue)

THUCYDIDES: I began my history of the war between
Athens and Sparta at the very moment the war began.
I believed it would be a great one, and more worth
writing about than any wars that had come before it. It
is of course inevitable that anyone involved in a major
war will think it is the greatest war that ever was, but I
do believe that this one will prove to be as important as
any which preceded it, and that its causes and its effects
will certainly not be resolved in my lifetime.

Of course the distinction men love to make between
times of peace and times of war is arbitrary, like most
distinctions of good and bad. One or other of the states
of the world are always at war somewhere. And though
we know that this has always been so and always will
be, we prefer to ignore this fact and to define the world
form the viewpoint of the state we happen to be born
in, and even to believe that at some future time we will
find some means of creating, for ourselves or at least
our children, what we like to call a 'Lasting Peace'. It is
not impossible that this is what our philosophers call a
contradiction in terms.

But it is also the reason why men such as myself venture
to write history, because we hope that perhaps someone
somewhere may learn from it. But this is not an easy
venture, for men are apt to accept all stories of the past
uncritically, and few of us will ever take the trouble
to find out the truth or even try to find it. The needful
euphemisms of political discourse in a city make the
cause and nature of any war a hard knot to untangle.
Eye-witnesses in particular are not always infallible, and
are apt to confuse what they remember with what they

7

need to remember. It is of course natural for men to apply the political and religious prejudices of the state we are reared in, and to make easy judgements about situations we do not fully understand, either because we are misinformed by our leaders; or because we don't really want to be truly informed of anything which might force us to think again.

I don't claim that you will accept all my conclusions, but it will be enough for me if my account is found useful by those who want to understand clearly what happened in the past, and which, human nature being what it is, will at some time or other, and in much the same ways, be repeated in the future.

(1. Pericles Addresses the Athenian Assembly)

The leading man among the Athenians at this time was Pericles. Under him the state was wisely led and at her greatest, for he showed them many useful things, like what is expedient in life, and what is just.

PERICLES: Athenians, I want you to see that behind this threat of war there is more at stake for us than there is for other cities.

I would ask you all to fix your eyes every day on the greatness of Athens as she really is, and to fall in love with her. Our ancestors, by their courage and their virtue, have given us a free country. To this inheritance our fathers have added a great empire. We do not copy the institutions of our neighbours, but offer a model to them.

In this city we do not say that a man who takes no interest in politics is a man who minds his own business: we say that he has no business here at all. Yet when our work is over, we are rich in recreations for our spirits. We enjoy games and plays and music; and in our own homes we find a beauty and a good taste which ease and delight us. And to all that we create and enjoy at home are added the fruits of our trade and empire, so that the good things from all over the world flow in to us.

Our superiority over other states derives from our democratic form of government, where all citizens elect leaders and vote at assemblies, and so share power. This is a more reasonable way of handling our affairs than the oligarchies, monarchies, tyrannies and dictatorships with which we are surrounded. But our system too is as liable to the same taints as any other. For we too, unless we are rigorous, may become confused by feeling that because our form of government is right, anything we do will inevitably be right also. So I would ask you to spend the emotive currency of our political vocabulary sparingly, and to try not to debase it by over-use. If you can manage to do this, future ages will wonder at you, and we shall have earned the right to say we were right, and to call our way of government the best in the world.

This depends above all on our relations with other cities, two of which have sent ambassadors to us on a matter of note. Let us hear them and act justly with them.

(2. Corcyra and Corinth)

CORCYRAN: Athenians, we have come to your noble
city to seek your help. Our own city Corcyra has
been invaded by Corinth. Corinth, as one of Sparta's
strongest allies, has attacked us, because we were
one of her colonies but have recently declared our
independence. If you do not help us we will certainly be
destroyed. Since Corinth has also sent her ambassador
here to contradict what we have to say, it would be wise
for each side to state their case quietly and fairly, so that
you can judge your true interests.

Athenians, you are the greatest naval power in Greece,
just as Sparta is the greatest land power. This is the
source of your security and your strength. Among the
rest of us there are only two comparable naval powers:
Corinth, who is Sparta's ally, and ourselves, whose navy
commands the western sea-routes which enable you to
trade with Italy and Sicily. So it is important to both you
and Sparta to maintain friendly relations with us.

But now Corinth has attacked us. Please understand
we are not offering ourselves as combatants. We only
seek your help against Corinth's aggression. What
their ambassador will argue to you is neither just nor
sensible. He will urge that we have no right to make
these proposals on the grounds that we are her colony.
It is true that our forefathers were Corinthians. But a
colony is not a subject state. The word is accepted by
all of us as meaning a new and *independent* city, founded
by citizens who have left their parent city. All who do
so will of course honour and respect their parent if they
are decently treated. This is something which you, as an
imperial power will appreciate better than Corinth.

CORINTHIAN: Athenians, the Corcyrans claim that we
are the aggressors and that they are innocent victims.
The truth is that we are only proceeding against them
after the grossest provocation. As an imperial power
yourself, you will understand that we did not found
colonies in order to be insulted by them, but to be
treated with proper respect. And your own colonies do
respect and honour you.

The Corcyrans are simply offering their navy to you as
a bait and are prepared to use it against Sparta if they
have your support. But you less than anyone can afford
to establish a precedent by which a power may receive
into its alliance the rebellious subjects of another power.
Since no one wants war, we are sure that you will share
our view that justice, wisdom and self-interest here are
one.

PERICLES: Both sides have made their points
persuasively, Athenians. But it would be madness to
endanger all this by allowing the Corcyran navy to
fall into the hands of Corinth, and so, effectively, of
Sparta, so I would urge you to support Corcyra against
Corinthian aggression with all appropriate means.

THUCYDIDES: As usual opinion in the Athenian
Assembly was divided, but Pericles' argument prevailed.
Corinth, however, still proceeded to put down Corcyra,
so Athens felt bound to fulfil her pledge.

(3. The Debate at Sparta)

The small Spartan Assembly, which consisted only of
a few ruling families, at once met to decide whether
Athens' support of Corcyra constituted an act of war

against Sparta itself. Corinth and Athens both sent representatives to address the meeting.

CORINTHIAN: Spartans, why are you still debating whether aggression has technically taken place instead of asking how best to resist it? For a long time Athens has been openly preparing for war. Now, in effectively seizing control of Corcyra, she has in effect begun it. You know the Athenian methods. They do this because they think you will let them get away with it.

Their great strength is that they act more quickly and adventurously than you. You think that any action may lose what you have got; they think that the farther they go the more they will get. In a word, they are by nature incapable either of living quiet lives themselves or allowing anyone else to do so. So make up your minds.

1ST ATHENIAN: Spartans, we did not come here from Athens to enter into a controversy with your over-excited allies. But since extraordinary verbal attacks have been made on our city, we would like to remind you of certain truths, to prevent you from making an unwise decision.

Remember what sort of a city you will have to deal with if you go to war against us. Our actions in the Persian Wars were for the common good; at Marathon and Salamis we faced the Persians single-handed, and saved Greece. We did not gain it by force. It was our fear of Persia which drove us to increase our power, and so our present allies came to us of their own accord and begged us to lead them. You yourselves were grateful to us. But when you and others grew less friendly, it became unsafe for us to let our empire go.

2ND ATHENIAN: Just as you, Spartans, have disposed
the affairs of your colonies to your advantage, so have
we done nothing unusual or contrary to human nature
in accepting an empire when it was offered to us. If you
attack us, you would soon lose all the goodwill which
you are now lucky to possess because others are afraid
of us.

1ST ATHENIAN: We know that things have gradually
gone wrong since the Persian Wars, but we believe that
nothing has happened which is necessarily fatal, and
which cannot be dealt with by reasonable discussion.

2ND ATHENIAN: Take time to decide this rightly. Think
of the huge part chance plays in war. You would be wise
to discuss our mutual interests before plunging into a
war which nobody wants.

1ST ATHENIAN: We urge you, therefore, while there
is still time to make sensible decisions, to settle our
differences by diplomatic means or by arbitration.

SPARTAN KING: Spartans, what is the heart of this
matter? Though the Athenians have argued shrewdly,
mostly in praise of themselves, they made no attempt to
deny that they are acting aggressively against our allies.

In the course of my life I have taken part in many wars,
so you must forgive me if I do not share the general
enthusiasm, nor think that war is necessarily a good or
safe thing. We must not delude ourselves with hopes of
a short campaign: I fear that we will bequeath to our
children many problems and much suffering that will
not be healed in our lifetime. We shall be engaged with
a people who live far off, a people who are wealthy and
well-equipped with ships and cavalry and infantry. Our

navy is inferior to theirs, and we have no public funds. We believe that money is unnecessary and invariably corrupts those who use it.

It is often said that we are a slow and cautious people, but that is nothing to be ashamed of. We alone in Greece do not become arrogant when we are successful, but in times of trouble we are like steel. We are not so highly educated as to look down upon our own laws and customs, and are too rigorously trained in self-control to disobey them. And we are not too clever in matters that are of no use, such as philosophy, or poetry, or rhetoric.

The Athenians believe that every problem can be solved by political means. But we are wiser, and know that though chaos and conflict may be postponed, they can never finally be prevented. In theory, politics is the art of controlling events. In practice, events happen first and politics is merely an attempt to undo harm already done. Athens' whole form of government is essentially self-destructive. When a whole people holds what amounts to a continual referendum on all decisions, they are quick to change their minds. This confuses their leaders, who spend more time on trying to handle their own people than on more important affairs. They are thus drawn into continual self-justification which takes the form of romantic declamation and patriotic noises. Both their politicians and their artists have some strange compulsion to proclaim that they are either in or making a Golden Age.

But we have no poets to delude us with such siren songs of what once was or what somehow will be. Our Spartan training is based on our understanding that war, though not lightly to be embarked on, is a natural state of mankind, since all human history shows that men clearly need it and even desire it. I would suggest that the Athenians talk of peace so often because they are painfully aware that they lack it within their own society. Peace is at best occasional. That is why we Spartans maintain a large standing army and avoid debates or electoral promises.

I do not suggest that we should do nothing. As the Athenians are prepared to submit to arbitration, we would put ourselves in the wrong if we declared war without further negotiations. Let us build up our sea-power, and let us borrow money to attract foreigners in the Athenian navy with offers of higher pay. Let us also foster revolts among their allies, for this will deprive them of the revenue on which their power is really based. Let us send to Delphi and enquire of the god whether it would be wise to go to war at this moment. And above all else let us send an ultimatum to Athens which would put us in the right when war begins, and give us more time to prepare.

(4. Spartan Ultimatum)

PERICLES: Sparta wants peace, and peace is still possible if you will give freedom to the states you have conquered or taken over.

Athenians, my views are the same as ever: I am against making any concession to Sparta. It is laid down by treaty that differences between us should be settled by arbitration. They have neither asked for this nor accepted our offers of it, and now they come here with an ultimatum which they know we are bound to reject. If we do grant what they call concessions, they will at once confront us with greater demands. Make up your minds what you want: either to give way to avoid pain, or to go to war to fight the Spartans and their Peloponnesian League until they are broken.

But before we go to war, I want you to remember that pride in your city must not be blind and uncritical, and I would ask you to think straight about two words you love and are apt to use too glibly. 'Right' and 'Wrong' are easy words to utter passionately, but less easy to use accurately. They are of course useful to justify and ennoble our human actions. But I doubt if such words deceive anyone but our allies, since the other states of Greece have heard us use them so often. The grounds of any war are usually ambiguous, so you should be wary of using supposed moral sanctions too freely, lest you do so on purely emotive or self-seeking grounds.

For the present let this be our answer to Sparta: that we will give our allies independence when the Spartans do the same with theirs, and allow them to have the kind of government they want; and though we will not ourselves begin a war, we shall respond to any attack with all appropriate means.

(5. Outbreak of War)

SPARTAN KING: Spartans, the Oracle at Delphi has spoken:

If you fight with all your might, victory will be yours.

Oracles, however are apt to be ambiguous, so we should insure ourselves against some hidden meaning behind Apollo's words. We should first consult our allies before deciding whether we should be the first to break the treaty and actually declare war. I should be glad to hear the views of the Corinthians, our chief ally.

CORINTHIAN: The oracle is simple and plain: the democracy of Athens is a tyrant state, and is bullying all Greece. So if we attack first, we will not be the first to break the treaty. The god, in ordering us to make war, surely regards it as already broken. Let us declare war at once.

THUCYDIDES: The Peloponnesian League then passed a formal declaration of war, with the promise of liberating all oppressed cities.

(6. Spartans at Acanthus)

The ensuing conflict proceeded fitfully. The two main powers rarely fought face to face. They preferred to use blockades, to lay waste territory or to occupy other cities by oblique means.

To divert Athens' attention from the main theatre of war, the Spartan General, Brasidas, marched as far as Acanthus, a small neutral city far north in Thrace. The Acanthians accordingly debated whether to receive him: on the one side there was the political group who had invited him, and on the other the people. But because it was just before the time of the vintage, they feared to lose the fruit which was still unpicked outside the walls, so they were persuaded to allow Brasidas to speak to them. He was not a bad speaker, for a Spartan.

BRASIDAS: Acanthians, the Spartans have sent me to uphold our pledge to liberate Greece. I am thus distressed to find that you have shut your gates against me, for I thought that we were coming to allies who welcomed us. It is not only the thought of your being against me which troubles me; others, to whom I am going, will think it very strange that you, whom I visited first, have failed to welcome me. This may make them suspect that there is something unreal about the liberation which I offer.

I assure you that I have not come here to harm you. My government has sworn the most solemn oaths guaranteeing the independence of whatever city which joins us. If we were to take sides in your internal affairs, Sparta would fall prey to those very vices of which we accuse the Athenians.

If now that I have made my position plain, you still say that you have friendly feelings for us, but are unable to help, or that you regard liberty as a risky thing to have, then I shall call upon the gods to witness that I came here to help you and could not make you understand, and I shall bring you over by force, and lay waste your land.

Please understand that in doing so I shall not be doing anything wrong. We Spartans have no imperial ambitions. We are only justified in liberating people against their will, because we are acting for the general good.

THUCYDIDES: After much debate the people of Acanthus decided to revolt from Athens, partly because they were swayed by the Spartan's oratory, and partly because they were worried about their fruit.

(7. Pericles' Last Speech)

2ND ATHENIAN: Athenians, our augurers have discovered disturbing omens, and reports from the war-front are ambiguous. Oracles with no authority are lowering our morale, and we are being devastated by plague within the city itself. It is clear that the gods are not with us.

1ST ATHENIAN: Many of us wish to challenge our government about the conduct of the war, and especially to question whether Pericles was entirely right to persuade us to it in the first place.

2ND ATHENIAN: He must shortly stand for re-election. But everyone knows that, regretfully, he is now a sick man.

1ST ATHENIAN: I fear it is necessary to review the whole situation.

PERICLES: Athenians, I knew it would be easier to persuade you to go to war than to maintain your spirits year after year. I know too well that public confidence is always fickle, so I see that I must remind you of your previous resolutions. Patriotism is not something to light inside you now and then, like a bonfire: it is a quiet flame, and continual, like the Olympic torch. It is because your own resolution is weak that you think my policy is mistaken. It is certainly a policy which entails suffering, but you must never, never forget that you are citizens of a great city and that for us death and happiness have always gone hand in hand. The man who is most truly brave is he who knows the meaning both of what is sweet and what is terrible in life, and who lives each day in that knowledge.

It would be easy for me to say golden and fiery things to you to cheer your spirits. But I do not offer you glib stimulations for the moods of the moment. I prefer to make you face the truth.

We are threatened with the loss of our empire through the hatred which we have incurred in administering it. But it is no longer possible for us to give it up, though you may think, in a mood of panic or apathy, that this would be a fine and noble thing to do. To those who say it was wrong to take it in the first place, I reply that now it would be more wrong and dangerous to let it go.

The right policy is what it always was: to endure patiently whatever the gods have in store for us, to face calamity with an unclouded mind, and to meet our enemies with courage. This was the old Athenian way, and we are still Athenians.

1ST ATHENIAN: I think the whole assembly must accept the weight of the General's arguments.

2ND ATHENIAN: I think we would all agree, but there are specific criticisms here which will only be satisfied after Pericles has paid a fine.

1ST ATHENIAN: I agree. But I would also like personally to propose his re-election, since we still believe he is the best man we have.

2ND ATHENIAN: I am glad to see the whole Assembly agrees with both of us.

THUCYDIDES: Unfortunately Pericles only survived the outbreak of war by two years and six months. Through his known integrity he had been able to respect the liberty of the people, and at the same time to hold them in check without flattering them. But his successors were less respected and trusted, and their conflicting manoeuvres often led to a loss of control. In a great city with an empire to govern, this naturally led to a number of mistakes.

(8. Mytilene Debate)

Mytilene, for instance, an ally of Athens, decided to revolt from her. Sparta was as usual slow in sending help and so the Athenians succeeded in crushing the rebels. In their anger, they voted that the entire adult male population should be put to death and the women and children should be made slaves. A ship was sent to Mytilene at once to put the vote into effect. But the very next day some Athenians became uneasy about this decision. Cleon, who had proposed the original motion, opened the debate. At this point Diodotus proposed an amendment.

CLEON: Athenians, I have often suspected that a democracy is incapable of governing others, and when I see how you are now changing your minds about Mytilene, I am convinced of it. Do you not see that to give way to feelings of compassion is a dangerous weakness which will not make your allies love you any the more?

You must face the truth. Your empire is effectively a dictatorship exercised over subjects who do not like it, and you will not make them obey you by injuring your own interests in order to do them a favour. People always despise those who treat them well.

There is nothing worse than to pass measures and then not to abide by them. Your ancestors and you are to blame for this by instituting and encouraging these competitive displays of rhetorical skill in the Assembly. You are more like an audience sitting at a play or the feet of a philosopher than a parliament.

You must learn to think straight. The truth is that if the Mytileneans were justified in revolting you must be wrong in holding power. But if you still wish to hold it then your interest demands that their revolt be punished by death. The only alternative is to surrender your empire, so that you can afford to spend time on philosophy.

DIODOTUS: I cannot agree that it is a bad thing to reopen questions of importance. Knowing that he cannot make a good speech in a bad cause, Cleon is trying to frighten you by misrepresentation and noise.

I am not so foolish as to try to sway you by pity or any abstract principles. But let us look at his claim yesterday that our decision will deter other cities from revolt in future. In human societies the death penalty has been laid down as a deterrent for many offences, yet men are rarely deterred and will take any risk to get what they want. Men and cities alike are by nature disposed to do wrong and there is no law that will prevent it.

Yet at present, if a city plans to revolt and realises that the revolt cannot succeed, it will try to come to terms with its enemy while it can. But if Cleon's method is adopted, every city will fight with greater determination, since surrender means destruction. Is that really in our interest? To spend money on a siege, and, if we capture the place, to find it in ruins so that we get no revenue from it? Even if the Mytileneans are guilty, we should pretend that they are not, in order to keep on our side that section of Mytilenean opinion that still supports us. So may I support Cleon in one particular respect, by inviting you to think straight? I propose that we cancel our decision by a show of hands.

2ND ATHENIAN: There seems to be an almost equal division of opinion here…

1ST ATHENIAN: Indeed, but the show of hands shows that Diodotus' motion is carried.

2ND ATHENIAN: Agreed.

1ST ATHENIAN: Then a second ship must be despatched at once.

2ND ATHENIAN: But the first has a twenty hours start.

1ST ATHENIAN: Then the second must row faster.

2ND ATHENIAN: I think we can safely leave that in the hands of the Mytilenean ambassador.

THUCYDIDES: The ambassador at once boarded the ship and urged the rowers on, giving them barley-cakes kneaded with oil and wine to eat as they rowed. Luckily they did not run into any adverse winds, and so arrived in Mytilene soon after the first ship. The original decree had already been read, but, to the relief of both sides, the counter-order was then read and adopted.

Not all colonies or allies were so fortunate.

(9. *The Melian Debate*)

SPARTAN KING: Spartans, it is reported that the Athenians have made an expedition against the island of Melos, which like other island states, has also refused to join their alliance, and wishes to remain neutral. Before attacking, the Athenians have sent representatives to negotiate. This is very much in our interest. We can expect no help from Melos, who are also a strategic threat to us, and since we have no navy to help them, we must leave the outcome in the hands of the Athenian negotiators and press on with our operations on land.

1ST ATHENIAN: Melians, we have not come to make set speeches to you, but calmly to discuss our mutual interests. We invite you therefore to say freely what you think, and to criticise openly whatever we may say.

MELIAN: That sounds very reasonable, and we agree that each side should put forward their views calmly. Yet what is scarcely consistent with such a proposal is the threat, indeed the certainty, of your making war on us.

2ND ATHENIAN: If you are going to spend the time voicing your suspicions about the future, or if you have met here for any other purpose than to face the facts so as to save your city from destruction, there is no point in our going on with this discussion.

MELIAN: You have invited us to say what we think, and it is natural that we should have different points of view. So tell us first what you propose.

1ST ATHENIAN: For our part, we will use no fine phrases saying, for example, that we have a right to our empire because we defeated the Persians, or that we have come against you because you have wronged us. We would simply ask you not to deny that you are a threat to us.

2ND ATHENIAN: We recommend that you try to get what it is possible for you to get. You will understand that a just outcome depends on one's power to enforce it.

MELIAN: Then in our view, since you will not allow us to speak of justice but only of expedience, we do think it useful for you, as much as for us, to maintain the principle that there should be just dealing between all states. Otherwise you might someday find your own fall attended by the most terrible vengeance.

1ST ATHENIAN: That is something you can leave us to worry about.

2ND ATHENIAN: Let us rather look clearly at your situation.

MELIAN: What would you suggest?

2ND ATHENIAN: We think you should surrender.

1ST ATHENIAN: This would save you from destruction, and enable us to profit from your resources.

MELIAN: You would not agree to our being neutral?

1ST ATHENIAN: No.

2ND ATHENIAN: You must understand that, if you remained neutral and if we remained on friendly terms with you, our subjects and other neutral states would simply regard it as a sign of our weakness.

MELIAN: But when they see what is happening now, surely the neutral states will conclude that in course of time you will attack them too?

2ND ATHENIAN: We are not so much concerned about the mainland states, but with islands outside our empire like yourselves who threaten our sea-routes, especially those who resent the needful restraint which our empire imposes on them.

MELIAN: But surely, if such violent steps are taken by you to keep your empire and by your subjects to escape from it, we who are still free would be foolish not to face you firmly rather than to submit to slavery?

1ST ATHENIAN: No, not if you are sensible.

2ND ATHENIAN: We are far too strong for you.

MELIAN: The fortunes of war are not always settled by greater strength. Your own past example against the Persians gives us hope.

2ND ATHENIAN: Hope is apt to be an expensive commodity.

MELIAN: Our position is difficult, and you may be sure that we know it. Nevertheless we have a kind of strength which you lack.

1ST ATHENIAN: We should be interested to hear what it is.

MELIAN: We are standing for what is right against what is wrong.

2ND ATHENIAN: Ah yes: men in a hard position generally say that. They do so simply to give themselves a kind of moral glow, rather than to define any reality. In our opinion, common sense is the sounder morality, and to ask oneself where one's interests lie is more useful than a generalised feeling that one is acting nobly.

MELIAN: Common sense suggests to us that what we lack in power will be made up for by our friendship with the Spartans, which is as much in their interest as ours. Past history also suggests to us that the outcome of war is full of surprises; and that since we are in the right, the gods are more likely to favour us rather than you. How a problem works out between states is never as certain as it may seem to either of them.

1ST ATHENIAN: So far as the favour of the gods is concerned, we think we have as much right to it as you have. Our beliefs about the gods and our knowledge of men suggest to us it is a necessary law of nature to rule wherever one can.

2ND ATHENIAN: As for your confidence that Sparta will help you, we would point out that though the Spartans are sound enough over their own affairs, their foreign policy is not especially dependable. Your Melos is an island, and we are in control of the sea.

MELIAN: We put our trust in the gods and in the Spartans. We will not surrender in a moment the liberty which our city has enjoyed for seven hundred years. We are sorry.

2ND ATHENIAN: We are sorry, too.

1ST ATHENIAN: And we would like to say that you seem unique in supposing the future more certain than what is before your eyes, simply because you would like it to be so.

THUCYDIDES: The Athenians immediately began to
besiege Melos. As there was some treachery from
inside, the Melians were soon compelled to surrender.
This time the Athenians did put to death all the men of
military age whom they took, and sold the women and
children of Melos as slaves.

(10. The Moral Climate)

In such ways as these, the whole Greek world grew
more liable to quarrels, convulsions and inevitably to
suffering. In every city the democratic leaders sought
help from the Athenians, and the oligarchical groups
called upon the Spartans. In the ensuing confusion,
human nature, never easy with the rigours of Law or
Justice, swept them aside, and surrendered to passion
and so to savagery.

Men speak, and even behave, nobly and sensibly when
they are not threatened. But when war interrupts the
economic benefits peace provides so conveniently, it
is apt to change men's character. Many turn to writing
invectives against the government, or try to reassure
themselves by recalling past glories or by dreaming
noble dreams of the future. And so it was at this time
in Athens, where plays and philosophical debate
abounded, and statues and great buildings were made to
give men and women a sense that that their city would
endure for ever.

Of course, it takes longer to make a fair thing than it
does to destroy it, and statues are particularly vulnerable
whenever political life is in turmoil. The night before
a large Athenian expedition was due to sail against
Syracuse in Sicily, most of the small religious statues

outside the temples and houses were mutilated and in particular, castrated. Some regarded this as an omen for the expedition, others as evidence of some other revolutionary conspiracy.

One of those blamed, perhaps undeservedly, was a young and successful general, Alcibiades, who had many lovers, especially one man who was little seduced by political passion, but who did try to influence affairs in his own particular way.

(11. Socrates)

ALCIBIADES: Socrates, why won't you enter public life?

SOCRATES: I try to influence affairs in my own way, Alcibiades.

ALCIBIADES: Athens needs you. And I need you, Socrates. Now.

SOCRATES: Indeed you do. And you know that I love you.

ALCIBIADES: And you know that I am eager to be your lover.

SOCRATES: But you need me now because...

ALCIBIADES: Because I'm about to make an important speech tomorrow to the Assembly about the expedition to Sicily. Against the Syracusans.

SOCRATES: Ah yes, the Athenian Assembly.

ALCIBIADES: I want you to help me with it.

SOCRATES: But you always laugh at me.

ALCIBIADES: Because the way you argue seems so ridiculous…

SOCRATES: Perhaps you are right.

ALCIBIADES: Yet you usually try to make me feel ashamed. Sometimes I think you are a god, and sometimes nothing but a satyr. You look like a satyr. But I see that your foolishness is a pretence to help you get what you want. It's a political device, and therefore useful.

SOCRATES: Ah, I see.

ALCIBIADES: You are in fact a bully.

SOCRATES: You're afraid I will bully you?

ALCIBIADES: I'm not afraid of anything.

SOCRATES: You are not an easy man to love, Alcibiades. You think you are foremost in Athens in family, beauty and stature, as indeed you are.

ALCIBIADES: But I am not content with myself, Socrates. Not yet.

SOCRATES: No, you want more honour and power even than Pericles.

ALCIBIADES: Of course.

SOCRATES: Excellent. And just as you hope to win power by proving yourself invaluable to the state, so I hope to win power over you by proving that I am invaluable to you.

ALCIBIADES: Good. I have come to you to learn.

SOCRATES: I doubt that. Don't you simply want a good tussle like most Athenians, who delight in games or war or winning arguments, but not Wisdom?

ALCIBIADES: *You* like to win arguments.

SOCRATES: Only if they are about Wisdom.

ALCIBIADES: That's why I'm here: to learn to influence people wisely.

SOCRATES: Ah, and on what subject do you hope to influence them?

ALCIBIADES: On anything which I know about better than they.

SOCRATES: Ah. Then you are a good adviser on things which you know about?

ALCIBIADES: Certainly.

SOCRATES: You know, if I recollect, about Writing and Harping and Wrestling, but not Fluting. Have I left anything out?

ALCIBIADES: No, not as far as formal education is concerned.

SOCRATES: Then are you going to influence them towards writing correctly?

ALCIBIADES: Of course not.

SOCRATES: Well, towards playing on the lyre?

ALCIBIADES: No…

SOCRATES: But at the Assembly they don't usually discuss throws in wrestling either.

ALCIBIADES: No, but…

SOCRATES: Then what will they be discussing?

ALCIBIADES: The war.

SOCRATES: You mean whether they ought to make war, or go on making war, and how?

ALCIBIADES: Yes. And when.

SOCRATES: And on whom it is better to do so?

ALCIBIADES: Yes. Like the Syracusans.

SOCRATES: And when it is better?

ALCIBIADES: Certainly, better.

SOCRATES: What do you mean by 'better'?

ALCIBIADES: I mean what is the best way to win.

SOCRATES: But mustn't you first be clear about the grounds on which you make war?

ALCIBIADES: You mean whether any war would be just or unjust.

SOCRATES: That's a good answer.

ALCIBIADES: I suspected that it would be.

SOCRATES: What do you mean?

ALCIBIADES: Because sooner or later you lead all discussions to that question.

SOCRATES: Well then, on what grounds are you going to advise the Athenians to make War now? And when? And how?

ALCIBIADES: That's interesting: for if we decided that we had to go to war with those whose cause was just, we could not admit it was.

SOCRATES: For then going to war would not be lawful?

ALCIBIADES: Well, not honourable.

SOCRATES: So you, too, will appeal to a sense of Justice in making your speeches?

ALCIBIADES: Oh, yes, one has to.

SOCRATES: To win the argument?

ALCIBIADES: Yes. And to do it better.

SOCRATES: You wish to make yourself better?

ALCIBIADES: Yes. But where am I to *begin*?

SOCRATES: With the injunction of the Delphic Oracle: 'Know Yourself'.

ALCIBIADES: That advice seems to me ambiguous.

SOCRATES: But suppose it rather said, 'See Yourself': have you not observed that the face of someone who looks into another's eye is reflected in that eye?

ALCIBIADES: I have been told so.

SOCRATES: Then an eye looking into another eye, will see itself?

ALCIBIADES: Maybe.

SOCRATES: Then look at me and keep looking.

ALCIBIADES: I am looking.

SOCRATES: I will show you such wisdom as I have.

ALCIBIADES: Won't you show me more than that?

SOCRATES: You always want too much, Alcibiades.

ALCIBIADES: I want all I do to be just and right.

SOCRATES: Very good.

But who first taught you to know what is just and right?

ALCIBIADES: Don't you think I might have found out?

SOCRATES: You might have, if you thought you didn't know.

ALCIBIADES: Well, I suppose that once I didn't know...

SOCRATES: Well said. When was that? Was it a year ago that you found out?

ALCIBIADES: No.

SOCRATES: So you thought you knew by then?

ALCIBIADES: Yes...no, I did know. Years ago.

SOCRATES: But years ago you were a child.

ALCIBIADES: Yes, I knew then.

SOCRATES: Ah yes, I remember when you were a child, while dicing or playing draughts, how you hit other boys on the head about that very question.

ALCIBIADES: I did?

SOCRATES: You said, very loudly and confidently, that one or other of them was cheating you.

ALCIBIADES: Well, he was cheating me.

SOCRATES: So you thought you knew, even as a child, what was just and unjust?

ALCIBIADES: Of course.

SOCRATES: But you've said that you did not know it by learning: so if you neither discovered it nor learnt it, how did you come to know it?

ALCIBIADES: I suppose I learnt it somehow.

SOCRATES: From whom?

ALCIBIADES: Well, from people in general.

SOCRATES: But do you find that 'people in general' *agree* with each other about what is just and unjust?

ALCIBIADES: No, that is the whole problem with the Assembly. Supposing our whole political form is wrong?

SOCRATES: That is why I avoid it.

ALCIBIADES: But I will have to work within it. If the Assembly is stupid and divided, how can I teach it to act justly? It is bewildering.

SOCRATES: Then if you are bewildered about things, how is it likely that you can know what is just, let alone persuade other people? You cannot teach things if you do not know them.

ALCIBIADES: But Socrates, the Athenians don't often discuss what is just or unjust. Politics is about what is most expedient.

SOCRATES: But is 'what is most expedient' the same as what is just?

ALCIBIADES: Well, sometimes. No, I don't think it's the same at all.

SOCRATES: Explain.

ALCIBIADES: Well, it depends on the intention behind it…and the situation, and…it is complex.

SOCRATES: Then I must try to help you. You think some things are expedient and others not?

ALCIBIADES: Yes.

SOCRATES: And again, some noble and some not?

ALCIBIADES: What do you mean?

SOCRATES: I mean, did any politician ever seem to you to be doing what was ignoble and yet just?

ALCIBIADES: No, never.

SOCRATES: Well, are all just things noble?

ALCIBIADES: Yes…

SOCRATES: And are all noble things good?

ALCIBIADES: Ah. No, I think some noble things are bad.

SOCRATES: What do you mean?

ALCIBIADES: Well, like when a man goes into battle for his country and is killed by his friend by mistake.

SOCRATES: You call that noble, in the sense that he is doing good for his country, but bad in the sense that the result is unfortunate?

ALCIBIADES: Yes.

SOCRATES: So it's not in quite the same sense that it is noble yet bad?

ALCIBIADES: Apparently not.

SOCRATES: So nothing noble, in so far as it is noble, is bad, and nothing ignoble, in so far as it is ignoble, is good?

ALCIBIADES: Apparently.

SOCRATES: Well now, are good things expedient or not?

ALCIBIADES: Yes...

SOCRATES: And are all good things just things?

ALCIBIADES: Certainly.

SOCRATES: Then surely you yourself have proved that expedient things are just?

ALCIBIADES: Socrates, you have bewildered me again.

SOCRATES: Didn't you yourself say it?

ALCIBIADES: No. Yes. No. I said you were a bully.

SOCRATES: Let us keep to the point. So if anyone says that bad things are sometimes just, what will you say?

ALCIBIADES: Socrates, I'm not sure what I would say or what I am saying now...

SOCRATES: What did you say?

ALCIBIADES: I mean I change my view as you question me.

SOCRATES: That is interesting…

ALCIBIADES: But Socrates, it is the nature of debate to change people's minds.

SOCRATES: And one's own?

ALCIBIADES: No, not one's own.

SOCRATES: Then it must be right to know one's own mind rightly?

ALCIBIADES: I only changed mine now because of the way you questioned me. You deliberately set out to trap me.

SOCRATES: I only tried to clear your beautiful but cloudy head.

ALCIBIADES: Well, all you've done is to confuse me.

SOCRATES: Really? Alcibiades, are you confused about cooking?

ALCIBIADES: Oh Socrates… I'm quite clear that I know nothing about it.

SOCRATES: So you're not confused about what you do not know, so long as you know that you do not know?

ALCIBIADES: Er… Yes.

SOCRATES: Excellent. Don't you realise that is the beginning of wisdom?

ALCIBIADES: No I don't. It would stop me going to the Assembly at all.

SOCRATES: Might that not be an advantage to everyone?

ALCIBIADES: It would be an evasion of one's duty as a citizen.

SOCRATES: You seem to be in the same confused state of mind as the rest who run our city.

ALCIBIADES: Why must you always try to complicate things? I am young and strong and can bring off whatever I set my mind to. Since the people who run the city are so stupid and such amateurs, my natural powers should see me through. Why need I go through a lifetime of questioning, which may or may not lead to wisdom, as you do, if all it does is to bewilder me? The more I am bewildered, the less fit I feel to enter politics.

SOCRATES: That too is interesting, is it not?

ALCIBIADES: Perhaps it's better, more expedient, and more practical to *feel* clear than to have deep knowledge and be bewildered.

SOCRATES: It takes time.

ALCIBIADES: But I have to speak as well as I can tomorrow when we debate our expedition to Sicily. All I want is to have a little more wisdom.

SOCRATES: To have Wisdom? You want to seize it, to own it. You want it for Power, not for itself.

ALCIBIADES: Do *you* not want it for Power?

SOCRATES: I have never wished to enter Politics.

ALCIBIADES: What is the use of building ideal republics in a philosophy group if you are not prepared to fight for them with the rest of us in the Assembly?

SOCRATES: I see that by temperament at least no Athenian is better suited for politics than you are. So I will help you to find Wisdom, but not to seize it.

ALCIBIADES: Well then, help me to find it. Come home to dinner and help me with my speech for tomorrow.

SOCRATES: It is not orations that cities need, Alcibiades, nor walls nor warships, but Knowledge, Wisdom and Virtue.

ALCIBIADES: You are naïve, Socrates.

SOCRATES: Perhaps you make me so.

ALCIBIADES: What is knowledge without cavalry? Wisdom without warships? Or even virtue if you are short of heavy infantry?

SOCRATES: It depends who controls them, Alcibiades. I see I had better go with you to dinner.

(12. Sicilian Debate in Athens)

THUCYDIDES: After a long debate in the Athenian Assembly, and in spite of some reservations about Alcibiades' character, it was resolved that he and Nicias should take charge of the proposed expedition against Sicily, where some of Athens' allies were under threat from the Syracusans.

1ST ATHENIAN: Athenians, the fleet is ready to sail for Sicily. Money has been voted to pay for our allies' help, and sixty ships are equipped and armed.

2ND ATHENIAN: But Nicias, our senior general has called a special Assembly to raise important questions.

Certain disturbing events last night have been brought
to the Assembly's attention.

NICIAS: I know that Alcibiades is delighted at having
been chosen for the command, because he naturally
hopes to gain profit and fame from his appointment. His
public conduct of affairs is often admirable, and he is
a fine soldier. But I am not the only one who is uneasy
about something in him which I find unsafe, unbalanced
and…undemocratic. Rumours are always suspect, but
it is unwise totally to ignore them. The blasphemous
desecration of statues scarcely shows the kind of civic
pride one expects in a serving general. I grant that
Alcibiades has a high and daring spirit. But you must
forgive me if I think it too high, and suggest that the
lawlessness of his private life does not persuade me that
he is a sound man for great affairs of state.

I would add, Athenians, that although we are indeed
ready to sail, we should still discuss whether we should
be persuaded by foreigners to undertake a war that is
not our business. I know that you are an adventurous
people and that no speech of mine could alter your
characters, but I would ask you, is this the right time for
such adventures? After all, a few years ago, I negotiated
a peace treaty which everyone for a while thought
sensible and effective. Yet now, under a specious
pretext, we aspire to annex not only Syracuse, but all
the states in Sicily. But even if we were to conquer them,
they lie too far off and are too numerous for us ever to
control them. The strain on our funds will be great if
we go and greater still if we stay there. The Syracusans
would fear us more if we did not go at all; or if we did,
to show our power briefly and leave as soon as possible,

since even our Sicilian allies will not be particularly grateful if we win, and even less so if we stayed there.

Athenians, I appeal for your support from the older men among you. Hold up your hands against this proposal, and vote in favour of leaving the Sicilians alone to manage their own affairs.

ALCIBIADES: Athenians, since Nicias has in all honesty expressed doubts about my fitness for command, you must of course examine the truth about me. I welcome this, because it is important, and expedient too, that we all act justly and wisely. So I am eager to stand trial at once to clear myself of these extraordinary rumours which Nicias has touched on. If every petty action is twisted into evidence of a revolutionary conspiracy, how can we act decisively in needful affairs of state?

What is this attack on me all about? Is it perhaps about actions which bring honour to our country, and profit, too? There was a time when Greece imagined that we had been ruined by the war. But they changed their minds when they saw the splendid show I made as your representative at the Olympic games, when I entered seven chariots for the chariot race and took the first, second and fourth places. Such things do bring honour, and if they are done with style they must also give an impression of power. But do you not think that to the outside world my achievements are a useful kind of folly, which bears witness to our strength and generosity and spirit?

Nicias himself does not question my military capacity, so why should he attack me? Do I criticise him? No, because I respect and admire him, and welcome his experience. Is it fairer for him to mistrust me because I

am young than it would be for me to doubt his capacity
because he is not so young? We can be sure that the
Sicilians will never join in united action against us. It is
more likely that many in the area will join us because
they hate the Syracusans. We have sworn to help those
who support us in Sicily, and it is our duty to do so.

This is the way we have won our empire; by coming
vigorously to the help of all who ask for it and by
striking first to avoid being attacked ourselves.
Remember what Pericles used to tell you: everything
soon wears out if it remains at rest, but in conflict it
constantly renews itself by fresh experiences, not by
speeches, but by action. Everything in life is dangerous.
But if we spend our time trying to avoid danger, we will
achieve nothing. Unless we grow we will decay. And
unless we live dangerously, we will soon cease to live at
all. Athenians, we must go to Sicily.

1ST ATHENIAN: Athenians, after hearing what
Alcibiades has so nobly spoken, I can see that you are
all even more eager to undertake the expedition.

2ND ATHENIAN: I agree. The vote would appear to
be unanimous. It would be unwise at this moment to
pursue the question of the statues.

(13. Debate at Camarina)

THUCYDIDES: The fleet set out at once and sailed
swiftly westwards, and the Athenians achieved swift
and substantial victories because Sicily was not yet fully
united. Accordingly, both Nicias and the Syracusans
sent ambassadors to those states in the areas which

wished to remain neutral or were undecided. In particular each sent envoys to the little city of Camarina.

CAMARINAEAN: Camarinaeans, before we listen to either side it is important that we clear our heads. At this moment you all detest the Syracusans because we have recently been at war with them, so Athens is of course hoping to make them allies against us. If however we were now to offer the Syracusans an alliance we would both be strong enough to throw the Athenians into the sea. Sparta has promised help to all of us in Sicily and they have much better soldiers than Athens. We should surely study carefully what our immediate and long term interests really are. But for now, we had better not keep the Athenian ambassadors waiting.

1ST ATHENIAN: Camarinaeans, we are not going to make you any fine speeches about our right to rule or our concern for freedom. We are here as much for our own security as yours. At this moment we both need each other's friendship.

2ND ATHENIAN: When you invited us to come here you acted very sensibly. You argued that it would be dangerous to Athens if you fell under Syracusan domination. You were right to fear them. So do not now mistrust your own argument.

1ST ATHENIAN: Our main motive here is the same as yours: fear. Fear of an aggressor.

2ND ATHENIAN: So accept our offer for your own sake and help us to put down Syracusan aggression.

1ST ATHENIAN: It is of course proper that you should first debate your fears and interests among yourselves.

2ND ATHENIAN: But you would be wise to decide
quickly, because Athens is expecting a quick reply, and
your position is not entirely trusted there.

THUCYDIDES: The Camarinaeans could not agree
among themselves how best to answer the ambassador
from either side. Some supported the democratic
speaker and others the aristocratic party. Since there
was no agreement they decided after a long and
inconclusive debate to send the same statement to both
the Athenians and the Syracusans.

CAMARINAEAN: 'Since Camarina has previous treaties
and trade agreements with both Syracuse and Athens,
we believe that we can only keep our oaths of genuine
friendship by allying ourselves with neither.'

I regret that this is the only wording which we have
all barely agreed that we can put our name to. It is not
satisfactory, and I suggest that we should now seek other
solutions. We should surely send secretly to Sparta,
inviting their help in some form, though it is by no
means certain that they will arrive quickly.

THUCYDIDES: I begin to suspect that those who govern
and seek to resolve hard problems, may end as King
Oedipus did, in finding that the answer to any oracular
question is not the one we sought, and that the poets
may be speaking accurately when they tell of a curse
working upon mankind, which the victim cannot
prevent or perhaps even recognise.

They have also told how Zeus long ago punished the
mighty King Tantalus, who discovered the secrets of the
gods and betrayed them to his children for the benefit
of mankind. So Zeus set fruits and drink just beyond

the reach of Tantalus' thirst and longings. He also set
a great rock over his head for ever to remind even his
descendents living today of a doom which no policy or
wisdom can in the end avoid. It is said that the rock and
fruits hang there still and among the wise it is feared
they will always do so. The myth is both useful and
relevant, though it is not one which is popular.

CAMARINAEAN: Then since all of us who seek to
prevent inevitable disasters are likewise tantalised, we
must endure as best we can, and pray that we be spared
from the general madness as long as the gods allow.

THUCYDIDES: When the Athenians and Syracusans
received the Camarinaeans' reply they both thought it
a threat to their interests and began to launch separate
attacks on the Camarinaeans themselves.

(14. Disgrace of Alcibiades: Debate in Athens)

In the meantime public opinion in Athens had become
increasingly convinced that the defacement of the
statues was part of some unidentified conspiracy. When
a conspiracy is once suspected, it soon becomes a
reality. Many were arrested, and one of them, to ensure
his safety, informed both against his associates and
others who were innocent. They were all tried and put
to death.

1ST ATHENIAN: Athenians, it is universally believed that
the man behind these plots is Alcibiades. Whether this
is true or false, he should be recalled from Sicily.

2ND ATHENIAN: But we should of course put ourselves in the wrong if we did not first hold an impartial investigation and follow all due processes of law.

1ST ATHENIAN: That is what I am saying. We should recall him, in the hope of vindication.

2ND ATHENIAN: I agree. That is what I am saying.

1ST ATHENIAN: Of course. But I would suggest that his urge to castrate religious statues at home does not indicate a sound state of mind for an Athenian commander in the field.

2ND ATHENIAN: We would be irresponsible to ignore the signs.

1ST ATHENIAN: No show of hands is needed at this point.

2ND ATHENIAN: Yes, I think we are all agreed that we must fetch him home.

THUCYDIDES: A ship was at once sent to Sicily in order to recall Alcibiades. When he learned of the Athenian prejudice, he felt it unwise to stand trial and accordingly set sail for Sparta, whereupon the Athenians condemned him to death by default.

(*15. Initial Athenian Victory*)

Nicias however continued to make a number of successful forays, and strove continually to keep his army in good heart.

NICIAS: It is no longer the time to debate what we are doing. This army of ours is a better ground for confidence than fine speeches. Let us leave that now to the gods on Olympus, who see more clearly than mortals, and get this war over as quickly as we can. We have already won a battle, but we need more money and cavalry, which I have sent for to Athens. We must be prepared for a war which will last some time.

(16. Alcibiades at Sparta)

ALCIBIADES: Spartans, I am grateful you have welcomed me to Sparta, though I realise you must be prejudiced against me. But as I am in Sparta, I will not try to seduce you with rhetoric and sophisticated argument. I feel much more at home here than among the Athenians with their perverse form of government, which I more than anyone have good reason to criticise. Yet since it was the official form of government where I was born I was forced for a while to conform with its absurd conventions.

On the subject of the expedition to Sicily I am even better qualified to speak. We sailed there to conquer the Sicilians, and after them the Greeks in Italy, and after that to attack the Carthaginian empire. These were our war aims; and the Generals who are left will, if they can, continue to carry them out. You should send Spartan troops and commanders to strengthen the Sicilians, and also intensify your diversionary attacks on the mainland.

Do not think the worse of me, if I join with my country's bitterest enemies. No. My love and longing for my country are so strong that I will shrink from nothing to restore it to its true nature. The man who genuinely loves peace, as I do, is the man who will fight the hardest to achieve it.

SPARTAN KING: Having heard all the points raised
by Alcibiades, who surely knows the facts better than
anyone, I propose that we send help immediately to
the Sicilians, and appoint a senior general to be its
commander.

(17. Nicias)

THUCYDIDES: The following winter, Nicias wrote to
Athens about the situation in Sicily.

NICIAS: Athenians, I have decided to tell you the exact
truth about our position and to ask you to come to
a decision about it. We, who thought we were the
besiegers are now the besieged. The Spartan general
Gylippus has arrived with strong reinforcements and
is forcing all who are still neutral to join him. He now
plans to attack our fortifications by land and by sea.
Do not think it strange that I use the words 'by sea':
Athenians, we no longer control the sea.

Our ships have rotted because they have been so long
in service, and we cannot drag them on shore to dry
and clean them, as the enemy now has more ships
than we have. We have had many problems and they
are growing daily. Food, forage and water have to be
fetched from a great distance; slaves are deserting; the
foreign seamen we pressed into service seize on the first
excuse to go back to their cities; some of our allies who
expected little fighting and large profits have deserted;
and some have even begun to take part in private
trading, which considerably impairs the efficiency of our
fleet.

I would ask you to either recall or reinforce us with
fresh forces and sums of money as great as those already
provided, and to send out someone to take my place, as
a disease of the kidneys has made me unfit for service.

THUCYDIDES: The Athenians refused this last request,
but voted in favour of sending out reinforcements.
Yet the Syracusan successes against the Athenians
continued, and after many battles, with victories
on either side, Nicias was finally surrounded, and
compelled to try to fight his way out.

NICIAS: No general likes making speeches when he knows
a campaign has not worked out as originally hoped
and planned. If he is wise, he knows that any words he
might utter are already spoken and pondered in the
hearts and minds of his men. So I will not offer you old
formulas such as 'Remember Marathon and Salamis'
or repeat that you are fighting for the great name of
Athens.

This is the truth of it. There are no more ships in our
dockyards and no more reserves of cavalry, and we
are trapped on foreign beaches and are far from home.
But Athenians, it is not walls or wealth or warships,
but men who make a city. So remember what Pericles
used to tell you, 'The man who is truly brave is he who
knows, in the self-same moment, both what is sweet and
what is terrible in life, and who lives and dies in that
knowledge.'

So let each man think of himself as a little city and hold
each patch of ground as if it was his own native country.
If you die, you will die for your country, and if we win
we shall learn from our mistakes and renew ourselves
for new ventures.

THUCYDIDES: Gylippus the Spartan also encouraged his men.

GYLIPPUS: Syracusans and allies, I do not need to speak to you with passion, for you already have it, and you know what you will surely achieve in battle today. For the first time the Athenians have found in you men who have stood up to the fleet which was the basis of their power. Remember that they came here to enslave your country, and would have committed atrocities against your men-folk and inflicted shame and dishonour on your women and children. Let us therefore go into battle angry, for anger as well as aggression is both enjoyable and just. In short, I offer you the greatest of all pleasures: vengeance.

THUCYDIDES: Both sides proceeded to man their ships.

When Nicias saw the size and nearness of the danger, he thought, as men are apt to at such times, that after all has been done that can be done, there is still something else to do; and that when all has been said, one hasn't said enough. And so he went round his commanders, repeating to them that their country was the freest and finest in the world. And he used all those words which men always use in such crises, and which without much change, spring from the lips of all who are human when they stop hiding their true feelings behind rhetoric and political language.

And so, not caring if their words sounded commonplace, they called upon their wives, their children and their native gods, passionately and loudly...and perhaps nobly. In the terror and confusion of such moments men always use such words because they believe that they will help.

And so when they have done what they can, men suffer what men must.

(18. The Spartan King Reviews the Victory)

SPARTAN KING: Spartans, it is always pleasant to celebrate a victory, provided that our lawful sense of patriotism is free of excessive emotion. We must all remember that no war-god, neither Athene nor Ares, is constant in their favours. But I am confident we shall win this war. When a people think they are invincible and are then frustrated, they lose their view of themselves; and the shock to their pride makes them more vulnerable than they would have been if they had not thought themselves superior in the first place.

Under such pressures it is good to have with us in Sparta such a man as Alcibiades. Let us honour him, for it is military clear-headedness alone which wins wars.

(19. The End of the War)

THUCYDIDES: Not long after, Alcibiades seduced the Spartan King's wife. Since she made no attempt to conceal her pregnancy, he thought it advisable to retire to Persia. A series of complex negotiations ensued, leading to Alcibiades returning to Athens, on condition that the democratic constitution was purified and restored. A new party was founded and Alcibiades was elected general. For eight years he fought successfully for his home city till he was relieved of his command after losing a battle at which he was not present. Fresh upheavals and surprises continue to arise daily in our city, and changes of side have grown more common.

When I perceive how the written laws and customs
of Athens are daily shifting and being corrupted, I
am content to live in exile. And when I wrestle with
the events I have lived through I feel like a man who
once thought himself some simple messenger in a play
by Sophocles and then found himself perplexed and
disturbed in the dark labyrinth of the Minotaur.

It is just possible – is it not? – that myth may offer a
sounder model of present reality than what I have here
attempted, and that even the greatest upheavals of
History should if searched thoroughly be regarded as
no more than timeless repetitions: new models of old
myths.

It may be argued that both myths and history are
politically useless because all events told of afterwards
are twisted in so many ways. But so is the verbal
coinage we live by. All words change their meanings
with time, and the high words which men use to try
to define political ideals may easily decline into their
opposites. Who knows now, even in Athens, what the
word 'Democracy' really means? Or what men really
mean when they use the word 'Justice'?

When the verbal currency of politics is debased by
orators, language itself is corrupted and devalued, and
men who are frustrated, angry, frightened and confused
strike out where they can…especially at easy targets
which annoy them.

(20. Socrates)

1ST ATHENIAN: Socrates, you have twisted words for many years to make the weaker arguments defeat the stronger.

2ND ATHENIAN: You have stood in the market place, insulted the government and corrupted men's minds, especially the young.

SOCRATES: Gentlemen, I have done none of these things.

1ST ATHENIAN: Then would you care to tell us what you actually *have* done? These serious accusations would surely never have arisen if your behaviour had been normal?

SOCRATES: You are quite right. I have been unfortunate, gentlemen, in gaining in this city the reputation for a kind of wisdom. Those who seek wisdom normally consult the God at Delphi.

DIODOTUS: The Oracle's replies are always cloudy.

SOCRATES: Yet one day it told a friend of mine that there was no-one wiser than I. This puzzled me, so hoping to disprove the oracle I consulted a man who was also highly respected for wisdom. But after questioning him thoroughly – he was one of our politicians – I found that although in the opinion of many, and especially himself, he appeared to be wise, what he said invariably turned out to be unwise.

So I began to question our philosophers, but found they could agree on nothing but that the other philosophers were fools. So I turned to the poets, both dramatic and lyric, and questioned them closely. I hesitate to say this, gentlemen, but any of you would have explained those plays and poems better than their actual authors.

So I then turned to our most experienced generals to learn the justest and wisest way to wage war. But they replied, 'Why should we be asked to explain what we are doing while we are busy doing it? We are trying to act wisely, but we would get on with it more quickly if you left us alone.' I thought that very fairly spoken.

So last of all I went to the historians, who perhaps have the advantage of only claiming wisdom about the truth of things already past. Each one of them spoke passionately and even wisely, except that they too did not agree among themselves about what had actually happened.

So perhaps the truth is that the oracle was not referring literally to me, but merely took my name as an example, as if to say, 'The wisest of all men is he who, like Socrates, at least knows how little he knows or understands.'

1ST ATHENIAN: Socrates, you say that *we* twist words, but we all know that no-one in Athens is more skilled at that than you. Experienced men such as ourselves know how to handle it.

2ND ATHENIAN: But you also do it to the young, which troubles and confuses them.

CLEON: So they simply go to bed with you, which is easier than arguing.

SOCRATES: Is that the corruption I am charged with?

1ST ATHENIAN: Of course not. We are civilised people.

2ND ATHENIAN: It is the corruption of minds that is offensive. By encouraging discussion about Ideal States, all you achieve is to make them feel superior to and critical of their government which does the real work?

SOCRATES: But surely everyone who governs us talks about political ideals almost continuously?

DIODOTUS: No, we both speak as practical men and avoid abstract statements.

SOCRATES: But I do not make statements: I merely ask questions.

1ST ATHENIAN: Socrates, if on this occasion we should not submit you to the due process of law, provided you gave up your perverse questioning and philosophising, what would you reply?

SOCRATES: I should reply to you, as I do to my sons, that I owe a greater obedience to God than to men. But not to go on searching the minds of others and myself day by day, that would be a life not worth living.

2ND ATHENIAN: Then have you anything further to say, before those who have accused you give their verdict?

SOCRATES: Only to urge you all to give me strict and true justice, provided you know, or even think you know, what it is. Do the best you can.

The Jury votes.

2ND ATHENIAN: It would appear that the jury unanimously finds you guilty of perverting the minds of the young. The death penalty will as usual be administered by the drinking of hemlock.

SOCRATES: Ah.

1ST ATHENIAN: But by the custom of your city you have the right to propose an alternative sentence. Have you anything to suggest?

SOCRATES: Well, as I have done no wrong, what do I deserve? If I had money, I could suggest a small fine: I suppose I could afford about five pounds. But if you really want me to ask for a just penalty, I would suggest free maintenance by the state.

2ND ATHENIAN: Socrates, the jury are all agreed that we should impose on you the penalty of death.

SOCRATES: I think that is pretty fair. And for myself, I should like most of all to spend my time among the dead in examining and searching people's minds, to find out who is really wise among them, and who only thinks that he is. Wouldn't you like to question Agamemnon, to see if he still held his war-policy on the subject of Helen really wise? Or Priam, to learn if he still thought it wise on religious grounds to take the wooden horse into Troy?

1ST ATHENIAN: Socrates, you really must ask no more questions.

SOCRATES: Ah yes, I forget that my questions frighten people. Come, members of the jury, you too must look forward to death with confidence. After all, the hard thing is not so much to escape dying as to escape from doing wrong. Trust that nothing can harm a good man either in life or death, since, whatever the poets tell us, his fate is not a matter of indifference to the gods. Well, now it is time we were going, I to die and you for a while to live: and which of us has the happier prospect is unknown to anyone but God.

He drinks the hemlock.

THUCYDIDES: As I write, the war still goes on.